OLE WAR SKULE
My STORY OF SATURDAY NIGHT

Written By: Joanna & John Darling Haynes
Illustrations By: John Darling Haynes

PRESENTED TO

_____

FROM

_____

DATE

_____

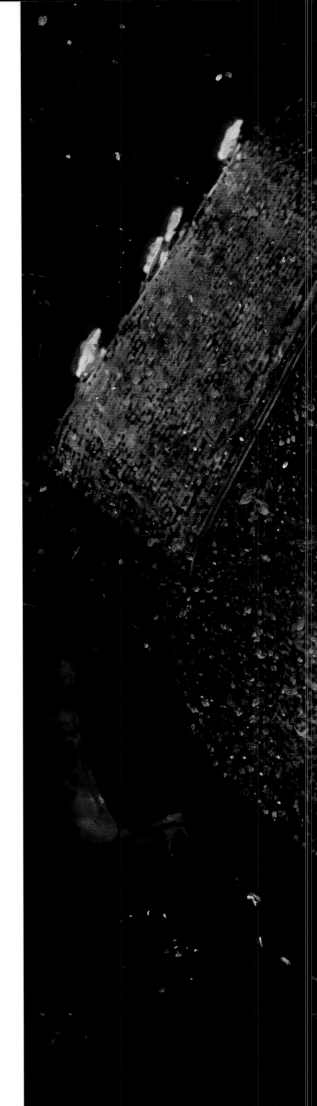

OLE WAR SKULE

THE STORY OF SATURDAY NIGHT

To Blue, Jackson and Allie
Love, Mommy & Daddy

Text copyright 2011
Joanna & John Darling Haynes

Illustrations copyright 2011
Joanna & John Darling Haynes

Designed by Jeremy Grassman

Milk Moustache Publishing

CPSIA LABEL: Production Date 10/07/11
Plant & Location: Printed by Lifetouch Production, Inc. in Kansas City, MO
Job / Batch # 63304

Special Thanks to:

Jady Regard

Herb Vincent

Abby Hannie

Rhonda Myer

Brian Homell

www.lsumovie.com

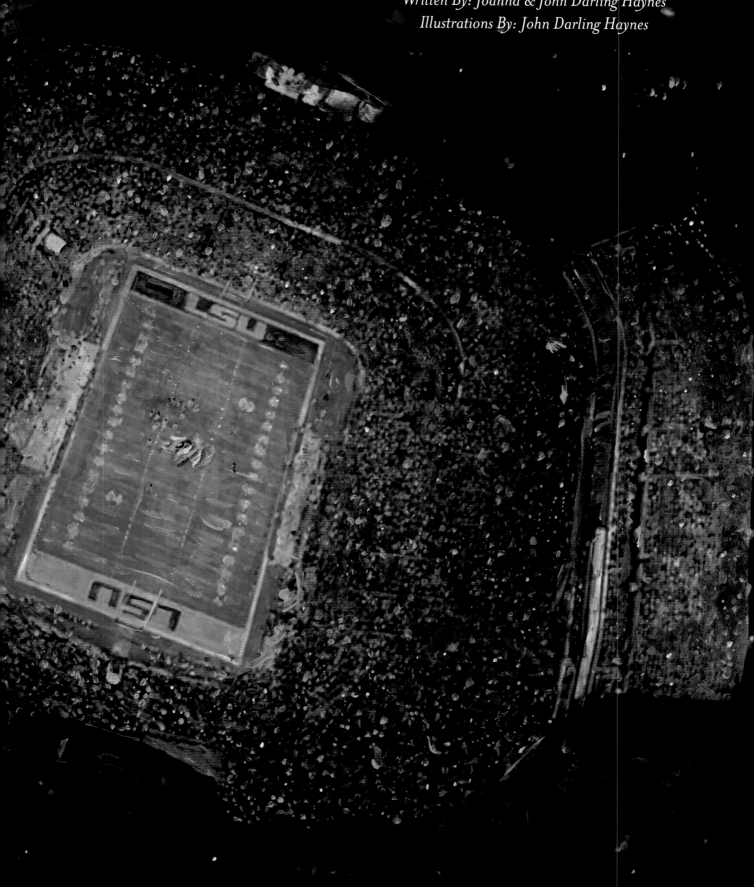

OLE WAR SKULE
STORY OF SATURDAY NIGHT

Written By: Joanna & John Darling Haynes
Illustrations By: John Darling Haynes

ONCE UPON A TIME...

...IN THE LAND OF HOT BOUDIN.

LOUISIANA STATE SEMINARY.

COL. S.H. LOCKETT DEL   CRESCENT LITH. N.O.

LSU opened it's doors in Pineville, Louisiana as the Seminary of Learning of
the State of Louisiana in 1853 before moving to Baton Rouge in 1869.

HISTORY WAS MADE AND TRADITIONS BORN

Artillery Drill — Firing.

General William T. Sherman was the institution's first superintendent. After the civil war he
donated two cannons from Fort Sumpter that currently reside outside of the military science building.

Baton Rouge

Pineville

Ole War Skule was a nickname given to the institution by the cadets becauuse of its military history roots.

Charles Coates

David French Boyd gave the university it's first colors – blue and white. Before playing the school's first collegiate football game in 1893, Coach Charles Coates, future Louisiana governor Ruffin Pleasant and several other teammates purchased ribbon on Third street and Main in downtown Baton Rouge to give life to the grey uniforms. The only ribbon available was purple and gold. The third color of Mardi Gras, green, was out of stock.

Tiger football traces its roots back to 1893 when the flying wedge formation was king and they nailed cleats to the bottom of their leather shoes.

LSU adopted their moniker from the "Louisiana Tigers," a brave civil war regiment made famous at the Battle of Manassas. New Orleans Zouaves and Donaldsonville cannoneers made up the fearless bunch of Louisiana soldiers. The Tiger logo traces it's roots back to the Washington Artillery of New Orleans.

THE GREAT TEACHER APPEARED

The famous four notes of Pre Game are taken from the tune "Tiger Rag." The dream started with 11 signatures and currently boasts over 325 members.

PRE-GAME ENTRANCE

MUSIC GAVE US A HEARTBEAT

The Golden Band from Tigerland began as the LSU Cadet Band in 1893.

The tradition of Saturday night football started in 1931.

LSU wore leather helmets up to the late 1940's.

The current Fighting Tiger logo decorating both sides of the helmet or "yellow hat" reflects a 1959 photograph of Mike the Tiger 1.

A PLACE BECAME HOME

Sheik was the tiger's name when he first arrived on campus in 1936. The students immediately voted to rename the live mascot after athletic trainer Mike Chambers.

The Fighting Tigers were crowned national champions in 1958. They were coached by Paul Dietzel who designed a unique three team system. It was made up of the White team, the Go team, and the Chinese Bandits.

OLE MISS VERSUS L.S.U.

L.S.U. STADIUM—BATON ROUGE

RESERVED SEAT

SEPT. 24, 1938

1959 LSU FIGHTING TIGERS

A LIGHT STARTED TO SHINE

The first live mascot in 1896 was man's best friend—a greyhound named "Drum."
1959 was the year that the Ballet Corps, now called the Golden Girls,
and the modern day costumed mascot were born.

FRIENDS BECAME FAMILY

LSU TD!!
vs Ole Miss 72 (One Second on Clock

16 OLE MISS	0:00	LSU	17
2 TIME OUTS LEFT			o
2 DOWN	10 TO GO	YD LN 10	QTR 4
WE'RE NUMBER ONE			

7 LSU 0:00 OLE MISS 3
2 DOWN 10 YDS. TO GO 4 QUARTER

Death Valley has seen it's share of historical gridiron moments such as the epic 1959 Ole Miss game, the clock stop game of 1972, and the earthquake game of 1988.

tober 08, 1988 winning touchdown U vs Auburn. In the last minutes of the football game the caused the stadium to vibrate so much that the signal was recorded on monstration instrument in the case. The instrument was located here in y that day. Note the largest signal. It is the winning touchdown.

Final Score 7-6

The Win Bar is a piece of the "H style" goalposts that were taken down in Tiger Stadium in the early 80's. It is tradition that all team members touch the Win Bar before running out into Death Valley.

It takes 150 gallons of purple, gold, and white paint to dress up Tiger Stadium before "It's Saturday night in Death Valley, and here come your fighting Tigers of LSU!"

The Fighting Tigers were crowned National Champions of the 2003 and 2007 seasons.

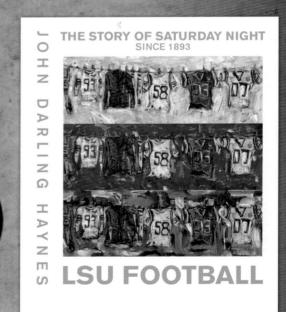

Prints by John Darling Haynes
available at: www.lsumovie.com

MY PHOTO ALBUM

MY LSU AUTOGRAPHS

MY LSU AUTOGRAPHS

MY LSU HISTORY

MY LSU HISTORY